50 Easy Vegan Cheese Recipes for Home

By: Kelly Johnson

Table of Contents

- Cashew Cream Cheese
- Vegan Cheddar Cheese Sauce
- Vegan Mozzarella
- Almond Ricotta
- Vegan Parmesan Cheese
- Vegan Cream Cheese with Herbs
- Coconut Milk Cheese
- Sunflower Seed Cheese
- Vegan Blue Cheese
- Spicy Vegan Queso
- Cashew Brie
- Vegan Gouda
- Vegan Ricotta Stuffed Shells
- Macadamia Nut Cheese
- Vegan Feta
- Vegan Parmesan Popcorn
- Vegan Camembert
- Tofu Cream Cheese
- Spicy Cashew Cheese Spread
- Vegan Swiss Cheese
- Vegan Baked Cheddar Dip
- Vegan Smoked Gouda
- Avocado Vegan Cheese
- Cashew Garlic Herb Cheese Spread
- Vegan Nacho Cheese
- Miso Cashew Cheese
- Vegan Creamy Goat Cheese
- Raw Cashew and Herb Cheese
- Vegan Pimento Cheese
- Smoky Cashew Cheese
- Cashew and Lemon Zest Cream Cheese
- Vegan Mac and Cheese
- Roasted Garlic Vegan Cheese
- Vegan Ricotta for Lasagna
- Vegan Cheese Ball

- Hemp Seed Cheese
- Vegan Cheese-Stuffed Mushrooms
- Vegan Caesar Salad Dressing with Cheese
- Vegan Cheddar Cheese Crackers
- Vegan Cottage Cheese
- Vegan Cheese Dip
- Vegan Cheddar Spread
- Raw Vegan Cheese with Spirulina
- Hemp and Cashew Cheese
- Vegan Cheese-Stuffed Peppers
- Pine Nut and Herb Cheese
- Vegan Parmesan Crusted Tofu
- Sun-Dried Tomato Vegan Cheese
- Cashew Mozzarella for Pizza
- Tahini Cheese Dressing

Cashew Cream Cheese

Ingredients

- 1 cup raw cashews, soaked overnight or for at least 4 hours
- 2 tbsp nutritional yeast
- 1 tbsp lemon juice
- 1 tsp apple cider vinegar
- 1/2 tsp garlic powder
- 1/4 tsp salt
- 1/4 cup water (or more for desired consistency)

Instructions

1. Drain and rinse the soaked cashews.
2. Place all ingredients in a high-speed blender or food processor.
3. Blend until smooth and creamy, scraping down the sides as needed.
4. Add more water if you prefer a thinner consistency.
5. Chill the cream cheese in the fridge for at least an hour to allow it to firm up.
6. Serve on crackers, bagels, or as a spread for sandwiches.

Vegan Cheddar Cheese Sauce

Ingredients

- 1 cup raw cashews, soaked
- 1 medium carrot, peeled and chopped
- 1/4 cup nutritional yeast
- 1 tbsp lemon juice
- 1 tbsp apple cider vinegar
- 1 tsp turmeric (for color)
- 1/2 tsp smoked paprika
- 1/2 tsp garlic powder
- 1/4 cup water (or more to reach desired consistency)
- Salt to taste

Instructions

1. Combine the soaked cashews, carrot, nutritional yeast, lemon juice, apple cider vinegar, turmeric, paprika, garlic powder, and water in a blender.
2. Blend until smooth and creamy, adding more water as necessary to achieve your preferred consistency.
3. Pour the sauce into a pot and heat over medium heat until warm, stirring occasionally.
4. Serve as a topping for pasta, nachos, or vegetables.

Vegan Mozzarella

Ingredients

- 1 cup raw cashews, soaked
- 1/4 cup coconut milk (or any plant-based milk)
- 2 tbsp nutritional yeast
- 1 tbsp lemon juice
- 1 tbsp tapioca starch (for stretchiness)
- 1/2 tsp salt
- 1/4 tsp garlic powder (optional)

Instructions

1. Drain the soaked cashews and place them in a high-speed blender.
2. Add coconut milk, nutritional yeast, lemon juice, tapioca starch, salt, and garlic powder (if using).
3. Blend until smooth, scraping down the sides as needed.
4. Transfer the mixture to a saucepan and cook over medium heat, stirring constantly, until it thickens and becomes stretchy.
5. Once thickened, transfer the mozzarella to a mold or container to cool and set in the fridge for at least 2 hours.
6. Slice and use on pizza or in dishes that call for melted mozzarella.

Almond Ricotta

Ingredients

- 1 cup almonds, soaked overnight
- 1/4 cup lemon juice
- 2 tbsp nutritional yeast
- 1 tbsp apple cider vinegar
- 1 garlic clove (optional)
- 1/4 tsp salt
- 1/4 cup water (or more for desired consistency)

Instructions

1. Drain and rinse the soaked almonds.
2. Place all ingredients in a food processor and pulse until crumbly.
3. Add water slowly until the mixture reaches a ricotta-like consistency.
4. Taste and adjust seasoning as needed.
5. Use in lasagna, stuffed shells, or as a topping for salads.

Vegan Parmesan Cheese

Ingredients

- 1/2 cup raw cashews
- 1/4 cup nutritional yeast
- 1/4 cup hemp seeds or sunflower seeds
- 1 tsp garlic powder
- 1/2 tsp salt

Instructions

1. Combine all ingredients in a food processor.
2. Pulse until the mixture resembles a fine crumbly texture.
3. Store in an airtight container in the fridge for up to 2 weeks.
4. Sprinkle on pasta, pizza, or roasted vegetables.

Vegan Cream Cheese with Herbs

Ingredients

- 1 cup raw cashews, soaked
- 2 tbsp lemon juice
- 1 tbsp apple cider vinegar
- 1/4 cup water
- 1/2 tsp garlic powder
- 1/4 tsp onion powder
- Salt and pepper to taste
- 1/4 cup chopped fresh herbs (chives, parsley, dill)

Instructions

1. Drain the soaked cashews and place them in a food processor.
2. Add lemon juice, apple cider vinegar, water, garlic powder, onion powder, salt, and pepper.
3. Blend until smooth and creamy, scraping down the sides as needed.
4. Stir in the fresh herbs.
5. Chill in the fridge for at least an hour before serving on crackers, sandwiches, or bagels.

Coconut Milk Cheese

Ingredients

- 1 can full-fat coconut milk
- 1/4 cup agar agar powder (vegetarian gelatin)
- 1/4 cup nutritional yeast
- 1 tbsp lemon juice
- 1/2 tsp turmeric (for color)
- 1/2 tsp garlic powder
- Salt to taste

Instructions

1. In a saucepan, combine the coconut milk, agar agar powder, and nutritional yeast.
2. Bring the mixture to a boil, whisking constantly until it thickens.
3. Remove from heat and stir in the lemon juice, turmeric, garlic powder, and salt.
4. Pour the mixture into a mold and refrigerate for 2-3 hours until firm.
5. Slice and serve as a cheese replacement for various dishes.

Sunflower Seed Cheese

Ingredients

- 1 cup sunflower seeds, soaked for 4 hours
- 2 tbsp nutritional yeast
- 1 tbsp lemon juice
- 1 tbsp apple cider vinegar
- 1 garlic clove
- 1/2 tsp salt
- 1/4 cup water

Instructions

1. Drain and rinse the sunflower seeds.
2. Place all ingredients in a blender or food processor and blend until smooth, adding water as needed for desired consistency.
3. Adjust seasoning with more salt or lemon juice if needed.
4. Use as a spread or in recipes calling for soft cheese.

Vegan Blue Cheese

Ingredients

- 1 cup raw cashews, soaked
- 1/4 cup coconut yogurt (unsweetened)
- 2 tbsp nutritional yeast
- 2 tbsp lemon juice
- 1 tbsp apple cider vinegar
- 1/2 tsp garlic powder
- 1/4 tsp salt
- 1/4 tsp onion powder
- 1 tbsp blue spirulina or activated charcoal (optional, for color)

Instructions

1. Drain and rinse the soaked cashews.
2. Combine all ingredients in a food processor and blend until smooth and creamy.
3. If you prefer a more "blue cheese" flavor, add a few teaspoons of miso paste or fermented soy sauce.
4. Chill the mixture in the fridge for a few hours to set and develop the flavors.
5. Serve as a dip, on crackers, or as a spread.

Spicy Vegan Queso

Ingredients

- 1 cup raw cashews, soaked
- 1/2 cup water
- 1/4 cup nutritional yeast
- 1 tbsp lemon juice
- 1 tsp garlic powder
- 1 tsp smoked paprika
- 1/4 tsp cayenne pepper (adjust to taste)
- 1/2 cup diced tomatoes
- 1 small jalapeño, seeds removed and finely chopped
- Salt to taste

Instructions

1. Drain the soaked cashews and blend them with water, nutritional yeast, lemon juice, garlic powder, smoked paprika, cayenne, and salt until smooth.
2. Add the diced tomatoes and jalapeño to the mixture and pulse until just combined, leaving some texture.
3. Heat the queso in a saucepan over medium heat until warm, stirring occasionally.
4. Serve with tortilla chips, veggies, or over tacos.

Cashew Brie

Ingredients

- 1 cup raw cashews, soaked
- 2 tbsp coconut oil
- 1/4 cup lemon juice
- 1 tbsp nutritional yeast
- 1 tsp apple cider vinegar
- 1/4 tsp garlic powder
- 1/4 tsp salt
- 1/2 cup filtered water
- 1/2 tbsp agar agar powder (for firmness)

Instructions

1. Drain and rinse the soaked cashews.
2. Blend cashews, coconut oil, lemon juice, nutritional yeast, apple cider vinegar, garlic powder, salt, and water until smooth.
3. In a saucepan, heat the mixture over medium heat and add agar agar. Stir constantly until it thickens and reaches a creamy cheese-like consistency.
4. Pour the mixture into a round mold and refrigerate for 4 hours until firm.
5. Unmold and serve with crackers or bread.

Vegan Gouda

Ingredients

- 1 cup raw cashews, soaked
- 1/4 cup coconut milk
- 1/4 cup nutritional yeast
- 1 tbsp apple cider vinegar
- 1 tbsp lemon juice
- 1 tsp smoked paprika
- 1/4 tsp turmeric (for color)
- 1 tbsp agar agar powder
- 1/4 tsp salt

Instructions

1. Drain the soaked cashews and place in a blender with coconut milk, nutritional yeast, apple cider vinegar, lemon juice, smoked paprika, turmeric, and salt.
2. Blend until smooth.
3. In a saucepan, dissolve the agar agar powder in 1/2 cup water and bring it to a simmer, stirring constantly.
4. Once dissolved, add the cashew mixture to the saucepan and cook over medium heat until it thickens.
5. Pour the mixture into a mold and refrigerate for 2 hours until firm.
6. Slice and serve as a vegan cheese alternative.

Vegan Ricotta Stuffed Shells

Ingredients

- 12 large pasta shells, cooked
- 1 1/2 cups vegan ricotta (see below for the recipe)
- 1/2 cup spinach, chopped
- 1/4 cup vegan mozzarella, shredded
- 1/4 cup marinara sauce
- 1 tbsp fresh basil, chopped

Vegan Ricotta

- 1 cup almonds, soaked
- 2 tbsp nutritional yeast
- 1 tbsp lemon juice
- 1/4 tsp garlic powder
- 1/2 tsp salt
- 1/4 cup water

Instructions

1. To make the vegan ricotta, blend the soaked almonds, nutritional yeast, lemon juice, garlic powder, salt, and water until smooth.
2. Preheat the oven to 350°F (175°C).
3. In a bowl, mix the vegan ricotta with chopped spinach, vegan mozzarella, and basil.
4. Stuff the cooked pasta shells with the ricotta mixture and place them in a baking dish.
5. Spoon marinara sauce over the stuffed shells and bake for 25 minutes, until bubbly and golden.
6. Serve hot.

Macadamia Nut Cheese

Ingredients

- 1 cup macadamia nuts, soaked
- 1/4 cup coconut yogurt (unsweetened)
- 2 tbsp nutritional yeast
- 1 tbsp lemon juice
- 1 tbsp olive oil
- 1/2 tsp salt
- 1/4 tsp garlic powder

Instructions

1. Drain and rinse the soaked macadamia nuts.
2. Place the nuts, coconut yogurt, nutritional yeast, lemon juice, olive oil, salt, and garlic powder in a food processor.
3. Process until smooth and creamy.
4. Chill the cheese in the fridge for at least 2 hours before serving.
5. Serve as a spread on crackers, sandwiches, or as a cheese dip.

Vegan Feta

Ingredients

- 1 cup firm tofu, pressed and crumbled
- 1 tbsp lemon juice
- 1 tbsp olive oil
- 1 tsp apple cider vinegar
- 1/2 tsp oregano
- 1/4 tsp garlic powder
- 1/4 tsp salt
- 1/4 cup water

Instructions

1. Crumble the pressed tofu into small, feta-like pieces.
2. In a bowl, mix the tofu with lemon juice, olive oil, apple cider vinegar, oregano, garlic powder, salt, and water.
3. Let the mixture sit for at least 30 minutes to allow the flavors to meld.
4. Use in salads, on pizzas, or as a topping for Mediterranean dishes.

Vegan Parmesan Popcorn

Ingredients

- 1/2 cup nutritional yeast
- 1/4 cup raw cashews
- 1/4 tsp garlic powder
- 1/4 tsp onion powder
- 1/4 tsp salt
- 1/4 tsp smoked paprika

Instructions

1. In a food processor, blend the nutritional yeast, cashews, garlic powder, onion powder, salt, and smoked paprika until it reaches a fine, powdery consistency.
2. Pop some popcorn and immediately sprinkle the vegan parmesan cheese over the warm kernels.
3. Toss to coat evenly and enjoy!

Vegan Camembert

Ingredients

- 1 cup raw cashews, soaked
- 1/4 cup coconut cream
- 2 tbsp lemon juice
- 1 tbsp nutritional yeast
- 1 tbsp miso paste
- 1 tsp garlic powder
- 1/2 tsp salt
- 1/4 tsp white pepper
- 1 tbsp agar agar powder
- 1/4 cup water

Instructions

1. Drain and rinse the soaked cashews.
2. Blend the cashews with coconut cream, lemon juice, nutritional yeast, miso paste, garlic powder, salt, and white pepper until smooth.
3. In a saucepan, dissolve agar agar in water and heat it over medium heat, stirring until it thickens.
4. Mix the agar agar mixture with the cashew mixture and cook for a few more minutes, stirring to combine.
5. Pour into a round mold, smooth the top, and refrigerate for 4 hours or until set.
6. Serve chilled with crackers or fruit.

Tofu Cream Cheese

Ingredients

- 1 block firm tofu, pressed
- 2 tbsp nutritional yeast
- 1 tbsp lemon juice
- 1/2 tsp garlic powder
- 1/4 tsp onion powder
- 1/4 tsp salt
- 1 tbsp olive oil

Instructions

1. Press the tofu to remove excess water and crumble it into a food processor.
2. Add nutritional yeast, lemon juice, garlic powder, onion powder, salt, and olive oil.
3. Blend until smooth and creamy.
4. Taste and adjust seasoning if needed, adding more lemon juice or salt to taste.
5. Chill for at least 1 hour before serving as a spread or dip.

Spicy Cashew Cheese Spread

Ingredients

- 1 cup raw cashews, soaked
- 1/4 cup water
- 2 tbsp nutritional yeast
- 1 tbsp lemon juice
- 1-2 tbsp hot sauce (to taste)
- 1/2 tsp smoked paprika
- 1/4 tsp garlic powder
- 1/4 tsp salt

Instructions

1. Drain and rinse the soaked cashews.
2. Blend all ingredients in a high-speed blender until smooth and creamy.
3. Taste and adjust the level of heat by adding more hot sauce if desired.
4. Chill for at least 30 minutes to let the flavors meld.
5. Serve with crackers, veggies, or as a spread on sandwiches.

Vegan Swiss Cheese

Ingredients

- 1 cup raw cashews, soaked
- 1/2 cup water
- 1/4 cup coconut oil
- 2 tbsp nutritional yeast
- 1 tbsp lemon juice
- 1 tbsp agar agar powder
- 1/4 tsp garlic powder
- 1/4 tsp salt
- 1/4 tsp turmeric (for color)

Instructions

1. Drain and rinse the soaked cashews and blend with water, coconut oil, nutritional yeast, lemon juice, garlic powder, salt, and turmeric until smooth.
2. In a saucepan, dissolve the agar agar powder in water and bring it to a simmer, stirring constantly.
3. Add the blended cashew mixture to the saucepan and stir continuously for 5-7 minutes until thickened.
4. Pour the mixture into a mold and refrigerate for at least 2 hours to set.
5. Slice and enjoy as a vegan Swiss cheese alternative.

Vegan Baked Cheddar Dip

Ingredients

- 1 cup raw cashews, soaked
- 1/2 cup nutritional yeast
- 1/4 cup carrot, chopped
- 2 tbsp lemon juice
- 1 tsp turmeric
- 1 tsp garlic powder
- 1/2 tsp smoked paprika
- 1/4 tsp salt
- 1/2 cup water
- 1/4 cup coconut milk

Instructions

1. Preheat the oven to 350°F (175°C).
2. Drain and rinse the soaked cashews. Blend the cashews with nutritional yeast, carrot, lemon juice, turmeric, garlic powder, smoked paprika, salt, water, and coconut milk until smooth.
3. Pour the mixture into a baking dish and bake for 20-25 minutes, until golden and bubbly.
4. Serve hot with tortilla chips or bread for dipping.

Vegan Smoked Gouda

Ingredients

- 1 cup raw cashews, soaked
- 1/4 cup coconut milk
- 1 tbsp nutritional yeast
- 1 tbsp apple cider vinegar
- 1 tbsp liquid smoke
- 1/2 tsp garlic powder
- 1/2 tsp smoked paprika
- 1/4 tsp salt
- 1 tbsp agar agar powder
- 1/4 cup water

Instructions

1. Drain and rinse the soaked cashews.
2. Blend the cashews with coconut milk, nutritional yeast, apple cider vinegar, liquid smoke, garlic powder, smoked paprika, and salt until smooth.
3. In a saucepan, dissolve the agar agar powder in water, then add the cashew mixture and stir until it thickens.
4. Pour the mixture into a mold and refrigerate for 2-3 hours until set.
5. Slice and serve as a vegan smoked gouda alternative.

Avocado Vegan Cheese

Ingredients

- 1 ripe avocado
- 1/4 cup raw cashews, soaked
- 2 tbsp nutritional yeast
- 1 tbsp lemon juice
- 1/4 tsp garlic powder
- 1/4 tsp onion powder
- Salt to taste

Instructions

1. Drain and rinse the soaked cashews.
2. Blend the cashews with the avocado, nutritional yeast, lemon juice, garlic powder, onion powder, and salt until smooth.
3. Serve immediately as a dip, spread on toast, or drizzle over salads.

Cashew Garlic Herb Cheese Spread

Ingredients

- 1 cup raw cashews, soaked
- 1/4 cup coconut yogurt
- 2 tbsp nutritional yeast
- 1 tbsp lemon juice
- 1 tsp garlic powder
- 1 tsp onion powder

- 1/2 tsp dried thyme
- 1/2 tsp dried rosemary
- 1/4 tsp salt

Instructions

1. Drain and rinse the soaked cashews.
2. Blend the cashews with coconut yogurt, nutritional yeast, lemon juice, garlic powder, onion powder, thyme, rosemary, and salt until smooth and creamy.
3. Chill for at least 30 minutes to let the flavors meld.
4. Serve as a spread on crackers, bread, or as a dip for veggies.

Vegan Nacho Cheese

Ingredients

- 1 cup raw cashews, soaked
- 1/2 cup water
- 1/4 cup nutritional yeast
- 2 tbsp lemon juice
- 1 tbsp tomato paste
- 1 tsp chili powder
- 1/2 tsp garlic powder
- 1/4 tsp smoked paprika
- 1/4 tsp salt
- 1/4 tsp turmeric (for color)

Instructions

1. Drain and rinse the soaked cashews.
2. Blend the cashews with water, nutritional yeast, lemon juice, tomato paste, chili powder, garlic powder, smoked paprika, salt, and turmeric until smooth.
3. Taste and adjust the seasoning if needed.
4. Heat the mixture in a saucepan over low heat until warmed through, stirring frequently.
5. Serve as a dip or drizzle over nachos, tacos, or baked potatoes.

Miso Cashew Cheese

Ingredients

- 1 cup raw cashews, soaked
- 2 tbsp white miso paste
- 2 tbsp lemon juice
- 1 tbsp nutritional yeast
- 1/4 tsp garlic powder
- 1/4 tsp onion powder
- 1/4 cup water
- Salt to taste

Instructions

1. Drain and rinse the soaked cashews.
2. Blend the cashews with miso paste, lemon juice, nutritional yeast, garlic powder, onion powder, and water until smooth.
3. Taste and adjust the salt as needed.
4. Chill for at least 30 minutes before serving as a spread or dip.

Vegan Creamy Goat Cheese

Ingredients

- 1 cup raw cashews, soaked
- 1/4 cup coconut cream
- 1 tbsp nutritional yeast
- 1 tbsp lemon juice
- 1 tbsp apple cider vinegar
- 1/2 tsp garlic powder
- 1/2 tsp salt
- 1 tbsp fresh rosemary, finely chopped

Instructions

1. Drain and rinse the soaked cashews.
2. Blend the cashews with coconut cream, nutritional yeast, lemon juice, apple cider vinegar, garlic powder, and salt until smooth.
3. Stir in the chopped rosemary for extra flavor.
4. Shape the mixture into a round form and refrigerate for at least 2 hours to firm up.
5. Serve with crackers, bread, or fresh vegetables.

Raw Cashew and Herb Cheese

Ingredients

- 1 cup raw cashews, soaked
- 1/4 cup water
- 2 tbsp nutritional yeast
- 1 tbsp lemon juice
- 1 tsp garlic powder
- 1/4 tsp onion powder
- 1 tbsp fresh parsley, finely chopped
- 1 tbsp fresh chives, finely chopped
- 1/4 tsp salt

Instructions

1. Drain and rinse the soaked cashews.
2. Blend the cashews with water, nutritional yeast, lemon juice, garlic powder, onion powder, and salt until smooth.
3. Stir in the fresh parsley and chives.
4. Shape into a log or ball and chill for at least 2 hours.
5. Serve with crackers, veggies, or as a spread.

Vegan Pimento Cheese

Ingredients

- 1 cup raw cashews, soaked
- 1/2 cup roasted red peppers, drained
- 1/4 cup nutritional yeast
- 2 tbsp lemon juice
- 1 tbsp apple cider vinegar
- 1/2 tsp garlic powder
- 1/4 tsp smoked paprika
- Salt to taste

Instructions

1. Drain and rinse the soaked cashews.
2. Blend the cashews with roasted red peppers, nutritional yeast, lemon juice, apple cider vinegar, garlic powder, smoked paprika, and salt until smooth.
3. Taste and adjust seasoning as needed.
4. Serve as a dip or spread on crackers, sandwiches, or vegetables.

Smoky Cashew Cheese

Ingredients

- 1 cup raw cashews, soaked
- 1/4 cup water
- 2 tbsp nutritional yeast
- 1 tbsp lemon juice
- 1 tbsp smoked paprika
- 1 tsp garlic powder
- 1/2 tsp salt

Instructions

1. Drain and rinse the soaked cashews.
2. Blend the cashews with water, nutritional yeast, lemon juice, smoked paprika, garlic powder, and salt until smooth.
3. Taste and adjust the seasoning if needed.
4. Serve as a spread, dip, or drizzle over your favorite dishes.

Cashew and Lemon Zest Cream Cheese

Ingredients

- 1 cup raw cashews, soaked
- 1/4 cup coconut milk
- 1 tbsp lemon juice
- 1 tsp lemon zest
- 2 tbsp nutritional yeast
- 1/4 tsp garlic powder
- Salt to taste

Instructions

1. Drain and rinse the soaked cashews.
2. Blend the cashews with coconut milk, lemon juice, lemon zest, nutritional yeast, garlic powder, and salt until smooth.
3. Taste and adjust seasoning as needed.
4. Chill for at least 1 hour before serving as a spread or dip.

Vegan Mac and Cheese

Ingredients

- 1 cup raw cashews, soaked
- 1/2 cup nutritional yeast
- 1/2 cup coconut milk
- 1 tbsp lemon juice
- 1 tbsp Dijon mustard
- 1/2 tsp garlic powder
- 1/4 tsp smoked paprika
- Salt to taste
- 4 cups cooked pasta

Instructions

1. Drain and rinse the soaked cashews.
2. Blend the cashews with nutritional yeast, coconut milk, lemon juice, Dijon mustard, garlic powder, smoked paprika, and salt until smooth.
3. In a large saucepan, heat the sauce over medium heat, stirring occasionally until warmed through.
4. Toss the cooked pasta with the sauce and stir to coat evenly.
5. Serve hot with additional nutritional yeast or herbs for garnish.

Roasted Garlic Vegan Cheese

Ingredients

- 1 cup raw cashews, soaked
- 1/4 cup nutritional yeast
- 2 tbsp lemon juice
- 1/4 cup coconut cream
- 1 tsp roasted garlic (or 2 cloves roasted garlic)
- 1 tbsp apple cider vinegar
- 1/4 tsp salt

Instructions

1. Drain and rinse the soaked cashews.
2. Blend the cashews with nutritional yeast, lemon juice, coconut cream, roasted garlic, apple cider vinegar, and salt until smooth.
3. Taste and adjust seasoning as needed.
4. Chill in the fridge for at least 2 hours to firm up.
5. Serve as a spread or dip for crackers, vegetables, or bread.

Vegan Ricotta for Lasagna

Ingredients

- 1 cup raw cashews, soaked
- 1/4 cup nutritional yeast
- 1/4 cup lemon juice
- 1/4 cup water
- 1 tsp garlic powder
- 1/4 tsp salt
- 1/4 cup fresh basil, chopped

Instructions

1. Drain and rinse the soaked cashews.
2. Blend the cashews with nutritional yeast, lemon juice, water, garlic powder, and salt until smooth.
3. Stir in fresh basil and adjust seasoning to taste.
4. Use immediately for lasagna or as a filling for other dishes, or refrigerate for later use.

Vegan Cheese Ball

Ingredients

- 1 cup raw cashews, soaked
- 1/4 cup nutritional yeast
- 2 tbsp lemon juice
- 1 tbsp Dijon mustard
- 1 tbsp fresh parsley, finely chopped
- 1/4 tsp garlic powder
- 1/4 tsp smoked paprika
- 1/4 tsp onion powder
- 1/4 tsp salt
- 1/4 cup chopped nuts (optional for coating)

Instructions

1. Drain and rinse the soaked cashews.
2. Blend the cashews with nutritional yeast, lemon juice, Dijon mustard, parsley, garlic powder, smoked paprika, onion powder, and salt until smooth.
3. Shape the mixture into a ball.
4. Roll the cheese ball in chopped nuts if desired, and refrigerate for at least 2 hours to firm up.
5. Serve as a snack with crackers or vegetables.

Hemp Seed Cheese

Ingredients

- 1 cup hemp seeds
- 1/4 cup nutritional yeast
- 1/4 cup lemon juice
- 1/4 cup water
- 1 tsp garlic powder
- 1/4 tsp salt

Instructions

1. Blend the hemp seeds, nutritional yeast, lemon juice, water, garlic powder, and salt until smooth.
2. Taste and adjust seasoning as needed.
3. Chill in the refrigerator for 1 hour to firm up.
4. Serve as a spread or dip for crackers, veggies, or sandwiches.

Vegan Cheese-Stuffed Mushrooms

Ingredients

- 12 large mushrooms, stems removed
- 1 cup raw cashews, soaked
- 1/4 cup nutritional yeast
- 1 tbsp lemon juice
- 1 tbsp fresh thyme, chopped
- 1 tbsp garlic powder
- 1/4 tsp salt

Instructions

1. Preheat the oven to 375°F (190°C).
2. Drain and rinse the soaked cashews.
3. Blend the cashews with nutritional yeast, lemon juice, thyme, garlic powder, and salt until smooth.
4. Spoon the vegan cheese mixture into the mushroom caps.
5. Place on a baking sheet and bake for 15-20 minutes, until golden.
6. Serve as an appetizer or side dish.

Vegan Caesar Salad Dressing with Cheese

Ingredients

- 1/2 cup raw cashews, soaked
- 1/4 cup lemon juice
- 2 tbsp Dijon mustard
- 1 tbsp nutritional yeast
- 1 tbsp apple cider vinegar
- 1 tsp garlic powder
- 1/4 tsp salt
- 1/4 cup water

Instructions

1. Drain and rinse the soaked cashews.
2. Blend the cashews with lemon juice, Dijon mustard, nutritional yeast, apple cider vinegar, garlic powder, salt, and water until smooth.
3. Adjust seasoning to taste.
4. Toss with fresh romaine lettuce and croutons for a delicious vegan Caesar salad.

Vegan Cheddar Cheese Crackers

Ingredients

- 1 cup almond flour
- 1/2 cup oat flour
- 1/4 cup nutritional yeast
- 1/4 tsp garlic powder
- 1/4 tsp onion powder
- 1/4 tsp smoked paprika
- 1/4 tsp salt
- 1/4 cup water
- 2 tbsp olive oil
- 1 tbsp apple cider vinegar

Instructions

1. Preheat the oven to 350°F (175°C) and line a baking sheet with parchment paper.
2. In a food processor, combine the almond flour, oat flour, nutritional yeast, garlic powder, onion powder, smoked paprika, and salt.
3. Add water, olive oil, and apple cider vinegar, and pulse until the dough forms.
4. Roll the dough between two sheets of parchment paper and cut into cracker shapes.
5. Place on the prepared baking sheet and bake for 12-15 minutes, or until golden and crisp.
6. Allow to cool before serving.

Vegan Cottage Cheese

Ingredients

- 1 cup raw cashews, soaked
- 1/4 cup water
- 1/4 cup nutritional yeast
- 1 tbsp lemon juice
- 1/2 tsp garlic powder
- 1/4 tsp salt
- 1/4 cup chopped fresh herbs (optional, such as parsley or chives)

Instructions

1. Drain and rinse the soaked cashews.
2. Blend the cashews with water, nutritional yeast, lemon juice, garlic powder, and salt until smooth but with some texture for a cottage cheese consistency.
3. Stir in the chopped fresh herbs.
4. Serve as a topping for baked potatoes, salads, or toast.

Vegan Cheese Dip

Ingredients

- 1 cup raw cashews, soaked
- 1/4 cup nutritional yeast
- 1/4 cup lemon juice
- 1/4 cup water
- 1 tsp garlic powder
- 1/4 tsp smoked paprika
- 1/4 tsp turmeric (for color)
- 1/4 tsp salt

Instructions

1. Drain and rinse the soaked cashews.
2. Blend the cashews with nutritional yeast, lemon juice, water, garlic powder, smoked paprika, turmeric, and salt until smooth and creamy.
3. Adjust the consistency with more water if needed, and taste for seasoning.
4. Heat the dip in a small saucepan over medium heat for 5-7 minutes, stirring occasionally.
5. Serve warm with tortilla chips, veggies, or crackers.

Vegan Cheddar Spread

Ingredients

- 1 cup raw cashews, soaked
- 1/4 cup nutritional yeast
- 2 tbsp lemon juice
- 1/4 cup water
- 1 tbsp apple cider vinegar
- 1 tsp garlic powder
- 1/4 tsp onion powder
- 1/4 tsp smoked paprika
- 1/4 tsp salt

Instructions

1. Drain and rinse the soaked cashews.
2. Blend the cashews with nutritional yeast, lemon juice, water, apple cider vinegar, garlic powder, onion powder, smoked paprika, and salt until smooth.
3. Taste and adjust seasoning as desired.
4. Chill the spread in the fridge for at least 2 hours before serving.
5. Use on crackers, sandwiches, or as a topping for vegetables.

Raw Vegan Cheese with Spirulina

Ingredients

- 1 cup raw cashews, soaked
- 1/4 cup nutritional yeast
- 2 tbsp lemon juice
- 1/4 tsp spirulina powder
- 1 tbsp apple cider vinegar
- 1/4 tsp garlic powder
- 1/4 tsp salt
- 1/4 cup water

Instructions

1. Drain and rinse the soaked cashews.
2. Blend the cashews with nutritional yeast, lemon juice, spirulina powder, apple cider vinegar, garlic powder, salt, and water until smooth.
3. Adjust the seasoning and consistency by adding more water or salt as needed.
4. Chill in the fridge for at least 2 hours to firm up.
5. Serve as a dip, spread, or topping for crackers and salads.

Hemp and Cashew Cheese

Ingredients

- 1/2 cup raw cashews, soaked
- 1/2 cup hemp seeds
- 1/4 cup nutritional yeast
- 2 tbsp lemon juice
- 1/4 cup water
- 1 tsp garlic powder
- 1/4 tsp salt
- 1 tbsp fresh parsley, chopped (optional)

Instructions

1. Drain and rinse the soaked cashews.
2. Blend the cashews and hemp seeds with nutritional yeast, lemon juice, water, garlic powder, and salt until smooth and creamy.
3. Stir in fresh parsley if desired.
4. Chill in the fridge for at least 1 hour to firm up.
5. Serve as a dip, spread, or topping for salads and roasted vegetables.

Vegan Cheese-Stuffed Peppers

Ingredients

- 4 large bell peppers, tops cut off and seeds removed
- 1 cup raw cashews, soaked
- 1/4 cup nutritional yeast
- 2 tbsp lemon juice
- 1 tbsp apple cider vinegar
- 1 tsp garlic powder
- 1/4 tsp smoked paprika
- 1/4 tsp onion powder
- 1/4 tsp salt
- 1/4 cup fresh cilantro, chopped (optional)

Instructions

1. Preheat the oven to 375°F (190°C).
2. Drain and rinse the soaked cashews.
3. Blend the cashews with nutritional yeast, lemon juice, apple cider vinegar, garlic powder, smoked paprika, onion powder, and salt until smooth.
4. Stir in fresh cilantro if using.
5. Stuff the bell peppers with the cheese mixture, packing them tightly.
6. Place the stuffed peppers in a baking dish and cover with foil.
7. Bake for 30 minutes, removing the foil in the last 5 minutes for a golden top.
8. Serve warm as a main or side dish.

Pine Nut and Herb Cheese

Ingredients

- 1 cup raw cashews, soaked
- 1/2 cup pine nuts
- 1/4 cup nutritional yeast
- 2 tbsp fresh basil, chopped
- 2 tbsp fresh parsley, chopped
- 2 tbsp lemon juice
- 1 garlic clove
- 1/4 tsp salt
- 1/4 cup water

Instructions

1. Drain and rinse the soaked cashews.
2. Blend the cashews, pine nuts, nutritional yeast, fresh basil, parsley, lemon juice, garlic, salt, and water until smooth and creamy.
3. Adjust the consistency with more water if needed, and taste for seasoning.
4. Chill the cheese in the fridge for at least 1 hour to firm up.
5. Serve as a spread on crackers, bread, or use as a topping for salads.

Vegan Parmesan Crusted Tofu

Ingredients

- 1 block firm tofu, pressed and sliced into 1/2-inch thick slices
- 1/2 cup vegan Parmesan cheese (store-bought or homemade)
- 1/4 cup breadcrumbs (gluten-free if needed)
- 2 tbsp nutritional yeast
- 1 tsp garlic powder
- 1 tsp dried oregano
- 1/2 tsp salt
- 1/4 tsp black pepper
- 2 tbsp olive oil

Instructions

1. Preheat the oven to 400°F (200°C).
2. In a shallow bowl, mix the vegan Parmesan, breadcrumbs, nutritional yeast, garlic powder, oregano, salt, and pepper.
3. Dredge each tofu slice in the mixture, pressing lightly to coat both sides.
4. Heat the olive oil in a skillet over medium heat. Sear the tofu slices on both sides until golden brown and crispy, about 3-4 minutes per side.
5. Transfer the tofu slices to a baking sheet and bake for 10-15 minutes, until crisp and golden.
6. Serve the tofu with a side of marinara sauce or a fresh salad.

Sun-Dried Tomato Vegan Cheese

Ingredients

- 1 cup raw cashews, soaked
- 1/2 cup sun-dried tomatoes, soaked and drained
- 1/4 cup nutritional yeast
- 1 tbsp lemon juice
- 2 tbsp olive oil
- 1/4 tsp garlic powder
- 1/4 tsp smoked paprika
- 1/4 tsp salt
- 1/4 cup fresh basil, chopped

Instructions

1. Drain and rinse the soaked cashews.
2. Blend the cashews, sun-dried tomatoes, nutritional yeast, lemon juice, olive oil, garlic powder, smoked paprika, and salt until smooth.
3. Taste and adjust seasoning as needed.
4. Stir in fresh basil.
5. Chill the cheese in the fridge for at least 1 hour to firm up.
6. Serve as a spread on bread, crackers, or as a filling for sandwiches.

Cashew Mozzarella for Pizza

Ingredients

- 1 cup raw cashews, soaked
- 1/4 cup nutritional yeast
- 1/4 cup water
- 2 tbsp tapioca flour
- 2 tbsp lemon juice
- 1 tsp garlic powder
- 1/4 tsp salt
- 1 tbsp olive oil

Instructions

1. Drain and rinse the soaked cashews.
2. Blend the cashews, nutritional yeast, water, tapioca flour, lemon juice, garlic powder, salt, and olive oil until smooth.
3. Pour the mixture into a saucepan and heat over medium heat, stirring constantly.
4. Once the mixture begins to thicken and become stretchy (about 5-7 minutes), remove from heat.
5. Use immediately as a cheese topping for pizzas, or allow it to cool and slice for sandwiches.
6. Optionally, bake your pizza with the cheese on top at 450°F (230°C) for 10-15 minutes.

Tahini Cheese Dressing

Ingredients

- 1/4 cup tahini
- 2 tbsp lemon juice
- 2 tbsp water
- 1 tbsp nutritional yeast
- 1 tsp garlic powder
- 1/4 tsp salt
- 1/4 tsp black pepper

Instructions

1. In a small bowl, whisk together the tahini, lemon juice, water, nutritional yeast, garlic powder, salt, and black pepper until smooth and creamy.
2. Adjust the consistency with more water if needed.
3. Taste and adjust the seasoning to your liking.
4. Drizzle the dressing over salads, roasted vegetables, or use as a dipping sauce.